HELP!
I Want
To Sell
My House

How To Sell Your House In A Recession

Andrew Dale

Copyright © 2013 Andrew Dale

First Edition 2013

All rights reserved.

ISBN:1481820796
ISBN-13:9781481820790

How To Sell Your House In A Recession

All the inside secrets revealed to get your property SOLD!

Disclaimer

The information contained in this book is from my own personal experience in the UK property market over a number of years. I have tried to convey as much information as possible to enable you to be successful and sell your property in bad times as well as good. I believe you can sell your property if you implement this information. However, I cannot be held responsible for any financial or other loss as a result of you trying to implement this information. I encourage you to take further advice from professionals and reach informed decisions for your own particular situation.

All the very best,

Andrew Dale

Introduction

Selling property can be one of the most stressful processes you will ever go through, and due to the recent economic conditions and downturn in the UK property market this can make it far worse.

It's true far fewer properties are being sold compared to 2006/2007, but if you look around there are still 'SOLD' signs on some properties, so how are they managing to sell?

A lot of properties are sold by other methods too, and these are not always methods you see advertised on boards in peoples' gardens.

This book goes into details to show you what is happening in the UK property market, and how you can make it work for you.

The purpose of this book is to give you a simple step-by-step guide to selling your property.

I reveal all the secrets of preparing your property, and helping you to 'show off' all its' selling points.

Along the way I give you continuous help and encouragement. You will hopefully laugh, and learn from the real life situations.

I have put together other peoples' real-life experiences and success stories to show how it can be done.

We have bought, renovated and sold properties over many years, and we reveal many techniques in this book.

If you use the information in this book it can give you an instant advantage over other properties on the market.

I have set out the information in easy to use sections, depending on how you wish to market your property.

Please read and take the first few steps on the road to success, and sell your property !!

CONTENTS

1	In The Beginning	1
2	You Can Sell Your Property	5
3	Unique Selling Points	13
4	Making the Very Best of Your Property	25
5	A Special Note On Apartments	55
6	Finding the Best Estate Agent	63
7	Setting The Right Price	85
8	Incentives	87
9	No Chain	91
10	Mortgages	97
11	The Viewings	101
12	The Surveyor	115
13	Property Auctions	119
14	Companies that Buy Houses	129
15	Raffle It	135
16	Swap Or Part Exchange	139
17	The Alternatives	145

Andrew Dale

Chapter 1

In the Beginning....

You have decided to sell your house or flat, probably for one or more of the following reasons:-

- You want to move to something bigger or smaller

- You need to move because of your job or new relationship

- Your relationship/marriage has broken up and you both want to go your separate ways and sell the family home

- You want to get your hands on the equity in the property to do something else with it. (i.e. either pay off debts or buy a place abroad etc)

- You have to sell because of major financial problems, and you are facing repossession at some point in the future

- You have got problems with neighbours or the area and that is affecting your health or mental well-being

These are some of the reasons why people come to the decision to sell either by choice or by circumstances forcing their hand.

So, you have previously thought, 'Do I really want to move?' and 'Do I really have to sell?'……….You have decided 'YES!'

That's why you have made the next decision and bought this book.

Let's make a start, now the following pages of this book are set out in different chapters, illustrating and revealing how you can sell your property.

If you read through the whole book first, and then go back and study the chapters that will be the most relevant for your property and situation.

All chapters are not totally independent of each other, obviously making your property look attractive is necessary for almost all cases.

But if speed of sale is paramount then the chapters on 'Auctions' and

'Companies that buy houses' are the ones to concentrate on.

If you want to try and get the full market value, and time is not as crucial then study the chapters on 'Property Competitions' and 'Estate Agents'.

You may find yourself pursuing more than one route, and there is no harm in keeping your options open until you have decided on the best method of sale for you.

Now lets first concentrate on the person who can and will sell your property, you already know them…….

It's YOU

Lets get 'You' up to speed ………..

READ ON.

Chapter 2

You Can Sell Your Property !

Be positive...

Yes, how many times have you heard that before, sometimes it's easier said than done, especially when you listen to the news on the TV, or read the headlines in the paper, all of which is telling you the 'Doom & Gloom'.

They are saying that house prices have fallen again, and the financial institutions are not happy about lending money......

......and so on.

Before you go and lie down in a darkened room let me tell you this......

Property is still selling, Ok not in the massive amounts we have seen previously, but people are still buying houses.

All you have to do is one thing.....

Sell Your House

That's it.

You bought it didn't you ?

Why did you buy it ?

Something must have made you think, yes this is it, this is right for me.

Now you want to sell it for whatever reason, so all you have to do is find ONE person who wants to buy it – Simple.

You are now probably an expert on your house, you will know more about it than probably anyone else, you have lived there, done all those odd jobs, and found out all the good (and bad) things about it !

Therefore, YOU are the best qualified person to SELL IT, and you can because it is special to you, you just have to use some selling ability.

GET FOCUSED

Write down on PAPER the GOALS as follows….

No. 1   Sell this house

No 2   Pay off debts

No.3   Move to …..

No.4   Go on holiday to….

No 5   Treat myself, my family to a meal at…..

When you do a simple list, the first item of selling your house is just a small part of your list of items you can do, once that has been done, the rest are just a matter of rewarding yourself for your success.

Regard selling your house as a challenge, a project, I am sure like most of us you have faced far worse situations in the past, and at that time you could not see a way out, or a possible way forward, and then as if by magic, and by your sheer determination and hard work you got through it, and surprised yourself at just what a remarkable person you are.

Keep believing in yourself, focus, picture that 'For Sale' sign outside your house, and see the same sign with that wonderful four letter word on it….SOLD !

Let me illustrate the following real life events for you to believe the power of your mind……

Roger Bannister, remember him, he was the first person to run a mile in under four minutes in 1954……the following year guess what….. many other people ran a mile in under four minutes….do you know why ? simply because up until that point they did not **believe** it was possible.

A great salesman I once met let me into the secret of his success. He had promised his wife he would be successful at his new job, selling insurance of all things. The first stage was to unplug the TV and cut the plug off, yes a little drastic you might think, secondly he stopped buying and newspaper. Despite the fact times were hard, and the other salesmen around him were struggling, he focused and would not allow any NEGATIVE vibes to keep shouting at him, he stayed positive and was the top salesperson within six months.

Believe and you can do it.

The second part is…….Sell Yourself

Smile, be friendly, be the best person your prospective purchaser has ever seen, you remember their name and use it, you shake their hand, you answer their questions, and you respond to anything the agent or their solicitor asks quickly and fully.

You are the personification of perfection, OK you say that's taking it just too far !

It's an act, call it what you will, but simply being pleasant, friendly, and willing to help is all I am asking you to do.

Let's put it this way, …………………..if I said to you I want to pay you £10,000, and in return I would like you to read two books and be polite, friendly, and as efficient as you possible can for probably a sum total of four or five hours, spread over three or four months, just in your spare time, would you be interested ?

Well, would you be even better at it for £ 20,000, and how good for £100,000 ?

What is the amount you will be left with after selling your house and paying off your debts ?

Usually, this should help you to understand that being the 'personification of the perfect person selling their house' really does pay.

Be positive, you only need one person, learn how to sell, and be the BEST !

A little note here

Two things that I really should not mention is Politics & Religion, and if you do not want me to mention one of them fair enough.. stop at this point NOW, and start on the next chapter instead!

If not, read on………

But if you don't mind me to mention just a little bit about religion…..here it is…. If you have any faith whatsoever, may I make the point of saying that belief in the presence of God, in whatever way you believe, and the act of prayer to ask for help in the sale of your property is not unreasonable.

Let's face it, you can do with all the help you can get, so a few prayers can do no harm.

Andrew Dale

Chapter 3

Unique Selling Points (USP's)

This is it…..this is one of the main points for you to understand, and once read please go and have a cup of tea, a walk around your garden and then sit down and read it again !

This chapter is absolute gold dust !!!!!

You need to pick out your properties USP's - unique selling points……………………..

If you think it doesn't have some then you need to give it some !

This will make your property stand out….

No….. not just stand out … it will put your property on a pedestal ready for someone to come along and say 'YES', I'll have to have that, don't let anyone else have it !

Still don't believe me...

Let me illustrate.....

What if you put your property up for sale at £ 1.00, do you think you would have someone round tomorrow with the money in their hand begging you to take it.... SURE you would, and you would probably have queue of people willing to offer you even more for it, in fact I would be in the queue waving a twenty pound note at you !!

You may not think you have much chance of selling your property, and I don't recommend you selling it for £ 1, or even £ 20 (although I would let you rent it back for a very reasonable rent !) but it was done to illustrate that there are ways for you to start thinking 'YES' I can sell this property, it's just how you think about marketing it and making it very much more saleable.

What we are going to do is make your property stand out, it will offer so much more value for money from other properties in your area, and in your price bracket.......... that it is a must have!

Does your property have......

A wonderful view, open land over countryside, or over a playing field, or a sea view or stream or river, this can be from any place in the property.

Does your property have a garden large enough for a decent game of football, for letting the family pets have a real good run, and safe enough to let your children play.

Have you already got some outbuildings or space for outbuildings or an annex to the property !!!

I for one, when looking at property tend to take special note of any agents details that state 'outbuildings' or 'granny annex' or 'room for a pony'.

It congers up images of brick out-buildings just waiting to have a bit of work, and you can have that home office you have always wanted or that workshop to do your DIY. You can finally store your collection of motorbikes that your wife currently objects to you dismantling every Sunday on the patio, and leaving those funny circles of oil here and there !

We all long for more space, peace and quiet, tranquility, for whatever reason, but I sympathize and any garden office or outbuilding for the kids, or family pets are a real bonus….. you certainly don't get those as standard on most new-builds offered by the developers.

Have you got a large garage or double garage, this can be ideal for a number of uses.

We tend not to put our cars in garages these days, not if we can find more useful things to do in them….

Extra room in the house, just needs converting.

Great for storage, or make do hobby room, it does not matter about the weather you can still play in the garage!

If you look around your area and see what other people have done with their properties, garage conversions, loft conversions, new garages…

Can you park several cars on your drive, have you got space for a touring caravan, boat and three cars!

If you have got a garage that you use as such has it got an impressive electric door?

A great idea for anyone who is slightly elderly and wants to keep their prized automobile in a locked garage.

The first few points mentioned are not actually telling you to have things built or moved but to use them and write down the possible uses to get any prospective purchaser to notice what an advantage they are.

Can your property be converted or altered from one dwelling into two without much work, is any old planning application still valid, even if the work has never been done, i.e. have you or the former owners got planning permission for an extension or loft conversion but not had the work done?….. this needs to be checked and is definitely a USP.

Extension or just a simple re-arrangement of your accommodation, and it can show it off at it's best..

Can you remove a wall between the kitchen and dining room, to make it more open plan, can you replace the window or door on the rear lounge with 'French Doors?'

That sound so much better on the agents sales details, and open up your lounge to that great garden.

If your garden is not so great, go and blow £ 150 on a trickling water feature from a garden centre, and stick it in you garden, it may be the best money you have ever spent!

You need to be flexible and examine your property bit by bit, again looking at what major developers do will give you some great ideas.

Is your property in a 'school catchment area' for a good school in the league tables!

That could sell it without question!

Is your property in a very quiet area, or an area of outstanding natural beauty?

Is it close to a motorway, or railway station?

Has your property got large rooms, high ceilings, character?

Is there a local Post Office (an absolute rarity these days!) bus stop, a park, or is it handy for a walk to the shops?

They may be obvious to you, but not to anyone gazing at twenty similar properties for sale.

Is your property an unusual design, or has it got four bedrooms instead of three, or a cellar etc?

Has it recently been............

Re-wired

Re-plumbed

Had new windows

New GCH

Is your property or garden low maintenance?

Or is it cheap to run, or does it already have any form of income from any source?

Your garden….is it a delight.

I remember going to look at a perfectly un-inspiring and dilapidated two bed terraced house a number of years ago, the only saving grace was the garden, it was clear that the little old dear who had lived in the property most of her life had 'green fingers' and although the property had been neglected the tiny back yard had been lovingly nurtured into an absolute 'oasis', 'a garden of Eden' amid a rather nasty jungle of poor houses and narrow forgotten streets.

Did we try and buy the property?, yes we did, the garden had sold us, hook line and sinker, to come home and sit there having a drink or our evening meal al fresco, and being able to unwind, it would have been paradise on earth !

(Unfortunately, a builder had take out some walls in the property a few years previously and the property was structurally unsound, and the mortgage company was not interested in how wonderful the garden was, no matter how many times we showed them the photographs!)

Anyway back to business, a garden with a fountain, rockery, decking, office, studio, workshop, (Large garden shed) it makes people interested.

Then the other things that you have probably heard mentioned a just a few hundred times on those property programmes on the T.V. like…

Original Features

If your property is not a new property they it will probably have some 'original' features like..

Coving, Dado Rails, Picture Rails, Ornate Skirting Boards.

Original Fire Places.

Ornate ceilings.

Original Ornate Tiling

Stained glass windows

Original Balustrade

This should be shown off wherever possible, because to create this type of work in a new house would cost a small fortune.

Bathroom & Kitchen

If you already have an impressive kitchen or bathroom or both these must be shown off to their very best, cleaned, de-cluttered and look like something out of 'Homes and Gardens' magazine.

Do you have a separate 'utility room' from your kitchen? Again it's on many women's 'wish list' so get it down on your USP list if you have one.

Remember these two rooms alone can make or break a sale.

Décor and Fittings

Anything about your property that you have already spent a lot of money on should be stipulated as a USP.

Carpets – If these are relatively new or in good condition they are normally a major expense, so make a point of recognising the fact to a prospective purchaser.

Wooden/laminate flooring – Very popular, easy for cleaning, low maintenance, ideal for pets and kids, a definite plus point.

Any rooms recently re-decorated.

Anything you are leaving behind, summer house, washing machine etc.

Real fire – many people have a 'real fire' on their wish list, particularly as it now seems a wonderfully economic and romantic way of heating. So have it burning unless it's in the middle of a heat wave.

Extra toilet, bathroom or en-suite

A great selling point for any home is extra conveniences.

On a wish list a woman likes to have a bathroom or en-suite she can spend some time in, and this is possible if there is more than one in a property.

Also, in modern living when two people are rushing to get ready for work in a morning this is an absolute gift.

Just having the words 'en-suite' on you property details makes it sound a little bit more special.

A further point on USP's

If you are still struggling to come up with some more USP's then invite one or two friends around to your home, preferably ones who may not have been before, and ask them what they like about it, and write down their responses.

Other people can come up with things you don't realise and don't notice because you are used to them. So it's good to get someone else round to see what they like.

If you are brave enough, the second part is to ask them what they don't like! This is not so easy, but it can help you to put things right that you didn't notice.

Chapter 4

Making the Very Best of Your Property

When people are first looking at buying a property most people, including myself would just drive past and have a look outside, and if I didn't like what I saw I may not proceed any further !

The inside may have been spectacular, but FIRST IMPRESSIONS are very important.

This is what is called 'Kerb Appeal', and you need to make sure your property has it in abundance!

Let's go through this one step at a time....

Get out a pen and paper and make a check list of jobs you may need to do, once you get started it's surprising how quickly you can make a difference.

The Approach

The street or road you live in, this is the approach to your property; this is what people are going to see BEFORE they even get to your property.

Is your area clean, is there street lighting not working, is there any abandoned vehicles, graffiti or anything that looks a mess?

Can you sort it out yourself; this is normally the quickest approach.

Clean up rubbish, clean off or paint over graffiti, abandoned vehicles get them moved.

Anything that makes your area or street look unattractive, it may seem fussy, but people are fussy about buying property.

The property next door, people viewing your property will look at the property next door also, now you do not want to fall out with your neighbours about their lack of tidiness, but if they have some abandoned rubbish in their front garden that has taken 'root', there is no harm in asking them if 'as an act of kindness', and 'as you are going to the local refuge disposal site', you can take it for them.

Alternately, if you are having a skip to get rid of your stuff, when you have finished, 'do they want to use the space left for the items they have? Free of charge as it seems a shame to waste it!'

The worst someone can say is no!....... most people are grateful for your help, because they may not have had the time or means to get their rubbish moved.

If your neighbour has a garden that has obviously been neglected, either because they are elderly or disabled, again you could just drop them a little note explaining that you have some time on your hands, and could pop round and tidy up, cut the grass etc. you could even charge a small amount for doing it. The key word here is HELP, you can help them, and it makes your neighbourhood look better.

This may seem a bit of a cheek, but you are helping yourself, and your neighbour as well.

Now to your property

Paint your front gate, so it looks shiny and new, oil the hinges so it does not squeak. If your gate is dropping to bits, then replace it.

Your front wall or fence should be clean and tidy, remove any weeds that seem to keep springing up on the outside of your garden wall. Any paintwork should be in good order, and any wooden fencing can be quickly rejuvenated with a coat of wood preserver if necessary.

Hedges, trees, bushes should be neatly trimmed, ideally any foliage that interferes with the view of the house should be cut back, gardens should compliment your property, not hide it.

If you have a front lawn then spend some time on making it look immaculate, trimmed, but not 'scalped' and water it regularly in summer months, a brown scorched patch of earth that use to be your lawn is not a feature you want.

Weed everywhere, any dead plants need to be removed, and make sure you have some colour and greenery. Go and buy a few plants if you need to, they don't have to be expensive just colourful, and eye catching.

Your front path should be clean and weed free. Any discoloured flags should be cleaned (I found the easiest & cheapest way was to go to your local supermarket and find the cheapest possible bottles of bleach you can, the unbranded ones, if you put this on your flags neat- i.e. undiluted, and just leave it for a few hours, or overnight, it cleans brilliantly, you don't even have to scrub them, yes you may need a trolley full of bottles, but it will still cost you less than ten pounds !)

If your front garden or driveway is a major eyesore, and a good clean and tidy is not enough, then the easiest and cheapest solution is gravel !

You should choose some 'small stone' gravel in a light 'buff' colour from your local DIY store or builders merchants, most will even deliver it for you, spread this out over damaged flags, or outdated crazy paving. If you have too much grass, and want to make more room for parking, you can cover the grass with an anti-weed material (Landscaping Fabric) you see in the builders merchants, and then put your gravel on top.

For the relatively small expense of gravel and little time it takes spread around, you will be amazed what a 'facelift' it can give to a garden.

(This is a favourite trick of many property developers!)

So your front garden or whatever bit of space is going to look great.

The front elevation of your property

If it needs attention, lets' have a look….

Your windows are "The eyes of the house"

Window frames should be clean, if they are UPVC there are some specialist cleaning products available for cleaning the grime and discolouration off the white plastic, and can make the frames look 'white' and new once again, available from any good DIY store.

Curtains, blinds etc should be clean and add to the exterior look. Net curtains that are not 'whiter than white' should be washed replaced or removed altogether. Look at your window panes themselves; they should sparkle in the sunshine!

If your window frames are wood and are tired looking, please repaint or re-varnish them.

If your property is rendered or pebble dashed, then this should be accessed, does it need any repair work, or can it just be repainted to make it look a lot better.

Your exterior colour scheme should be in-keeping with the property, and other surrounding properties.

Walk around your local area and pick up ideas from similar properties, even taking a few snap shots of the best looking properties, try and pick out the ideas that make the biggest differences, but are relatively easy and inexpensive to do.

White paintwork for the window frames, or brown wood stain, then cream, magnolia, or white is best for any render.

Outside redecoration can be a bit daunting for even some DIY enthusiasts, so it may be necessary to call in the professionals. However, if you want to do it yourself, but it is the thought of clinging to some step ladder for hours that puts you off, it can be much easier hiring a 'cherry picker' yes, a hydraulic platform that can easily take you from ground level to more or less any height, plus you can take up all your tools and paint as well.

I used a 'cherry picker' a number of years ago instead of ladders because it was safer, and now I would always try and use one providing there is access for it at the property. They are very easy to operate and much quicker to use, just check the weather forecast first!

Whilst you have the equipment, now is the time to check the roof, and clean out the gutters. Do the same at the back and sides of your property, but remember the front is the most important.

You should stay to 'safe' colours for your property, both inside and out.

It's a bit like 'custom cars', yes we do notice them, and stare in amazement, but how many of us buy them? ……exactly……..not many!

Any bright or outlandish colours need to go, we are trying to sell your property, not make it stand out for all the wrong reasons.

Having said that the one place where colour is allowed is the front door, here red or blue is best. Anything else on the front door, like a letter box, key hole, or 'Yale' type lock, house number and door knocker should be either highly polished or replaced with new.

A door bell that looks attractive and works, there is nothing worse than keeping a viewer on the front doorstep for five minutes, just because your door bell does not work.

A reasonable sized bush, or potted specimen plant either side of your front door to frame the entrance is a must, providing you have some space.

If not then some hanging baskets or even an ornamental outside light, one either side of your front door can add to the look. Even 'solar powered' ones that are inexpensive and take no wiring up can do the trick.

Window boxes can also be a stunning addition to the front of any house, especially if there is a very small front garden, or your property style is rather uninspiring.

You should make sure the number of your house is clearly visible, and put the number on the gate post as well if necessary, but please use some numbers that are ready made, or a small plaque, some hastily 'daubed' number in white paint, that has run slightly, does not help to create the right impression!

Give it a name

Give your property a name, it can still have a number, but a name on the agents details makes it a little bit more special, so a much more pleasing impression can be gained from calling it...

'Rose Cottage'

'Mansion House'

'The Cedars'

'Ocean View'

They give a picture in your mind of an idyllic place to live, or simply adding a word to the name of the road you live in, for instance...

If you live in a road called 'Park Road' you could just call your property 'Park House', signifying it is the main property on that road, or if someone has already done that with their house, call yours 'Park Manor', do you see what we are trying to do ?

You can put this on a plaque next to your front door, or have some vinyl letters made to put on the glass over your front door…..available to order at a very reasonable cost from any print & copy shop.

Inside your property

Please go and visit one or two new show homes that are for sale, show homes will show you how it is done, and take some snapshots. You will notice show homes don't have many items of furniture, and what furniture they do have is rather small.

It is very important all your personal items, photographs, ornaments, collections of memorabilia etc should all be removed, packed away out of sight. A viewer should be able to imagine themselves owning the property, and having all your personal possessions everywhere is not going to help this at all. Now is a good time to have a sort out, any unwanted items you can sell, do a car boot, or donate to a charity shop. Then you will have fewer items to pack away, and less to move to your next home.

I'm sure you have heard it before about colour schemes, but here we go again, neutral colours, beige, cream, magnolia etc. Nothing offensive! If you are not sure what neutral colour to choose I would recommend WHITE matt emulsion, at least to start with, and then you could be a bit braver on one wall with beige, or a very pale green, blue or yellow!

Arrange each room to be the best it can be, and focus on the purpose of that room, don't leave the prospective viewer wondering what they can do with it, some people don't have much imagination, it is your job to extol the virtues of every square meter of your property.

Hallway

Clear away **EVERYTHING** from your hallway, yes everything.

Put all your coats, shoes, umbrellas etc away in cupboards, don't leave them on display in the hallway. Hallway furniture is usually too much, if you have to have something for the telephone to go on, make it as small as possible.

The colour should be light and neutral, if it is dark and dismal, repaint it now.

Put up a large mirror, and perhaps one or two pictures, no more.

If there is room, a vase of real flowers, or good looking pot plant should be installed, in a corner, so as not to take up unnecessary space. I have found a large red floor standing vase with colourful artificial poppies & lillies always looks good, and does not need watering !

Any hall carpet should be clean; any wear and tear can be hidden by a decent door mat or tasteful rug in the hallway. You can hire a carpet cleaner and do it yourself, or get someone in to do it for you.

A hallway is one of the best candidates for wooden flooring, or laminate flooring. If the original floorboards are in good condition it may be easier & more of a sales feature to just uncover them and give them a coat of varnish.

Most hallways are relatively small and narrow and it is relatively easy and inexpensive to put down a light coloured laminate floor. This will be a massive boost to the light in the hallway, and is practical to cope with all the foot traffic, especially in bad weather.

If the hallway still appears dark, have you tried painting the ceiling in white emulsion and increasing the wattage of any light bulbs to the maximum you can use in its fitting? (Energy efficient light bulbs are excellent, but where you need a large amount of light, possibly go back to more standard bulbs if you can, or change to a chandelier for greater effect)

Any original features like coving or banisters with spindles should be shown off at their best, any older properties that seem to not have spindles on the stairs may need a closer inspection, if they were 'boxed in' simply removing the panelling can expose some amazing features. This is the same for interior doors, and fireplaces, original features that are there, but hidden can simply be shown off normally without too much effort. Prospective purchasers see original features as a bonus, even if they are not to your personal taste.

The Lounge

This is the main focus of where you live, this should have a feeling of space, relaxation, and a 'touch of class'.

The windows and any patio doors in your living room should be unobstructed, try to arrange furniture so viewers can walk up to them and look out without having to walk around any obstacles.

Curtains either side of the windows and patio doors help to frame the view beyond, they should ideally match in with the colour of your soft furnishings in the room.

Look at your furniture, does there seem too much of it?

Is it too big for the size of the room?

Any large chunky pieces of furniture should be removed if they take over the room.

Look around your other rooms for any items of furniture that are more ornate, or decorative, try them in your lounge, move the furniture around as many times as you want until it works better.

Any old or tatty sofas or chairs can be covered with new ready made covers, or loose throws, and the addition of some new colourful cushions can work wonders. If you still think it needs more than that get rid of it and start again.

The lounge is the best candidate for a large coloured rug, it is definitely worth it and can be taken with you when you move!

The fireplace is an obvious focal point, but it should not completely dominate the room, some large older dark coloured fireplaces can be toned down with painting it in a lighter colour.

Any old fashioned gas fire can be hidden behind a decorative fire guard, or should be replaced, or taken out and the space suitably filled with something ornamental like flowers, candles, or the like.

Have a large mirror over the fireplace, and a 'companion set' (brush, shovel & poker) on the hearth, even if it is not a real fire.

So, no clutter, some colour, no evidence of pets or children !

Your lounge is spacious, relaxing and elegant.

The Dining Room

You may not have a separate dining room, but you should have space somewhere in your property to have a table and chairs, perhaps in a corner of your lounge, or kitchen.

This needs to be defined as dining space, even if you have never used it as such.

Make sure the table surface is clean and in good condition. If all else fails cover it with a spotless tablecloth.

Fresh flowers in the centre of the dining table and having the table set out formally with some nice cutlery can add a touch of class, with some red napkins and candles.

If the room or space you have for the dining table is relatively small then remove some of the chairs, or try the table with one edge against a wall. If this still does not work consider buying a smaller table. A round table is easier to locate and if it is glass it gives the appearance of more space.

A dining area or room looks better with one or two pictures on the wall and preferably a mirror.

The rest of the area should be de-cluttered.

Definitely no food and no tomato sauce bottles anywhere in sight!

Kitchen

This used to be a place where you just did the cooking….. but not any more, this is probably the number one room in the house in terms of style, the bathroom coming a close second.

The kitchen can be the make or break room, it can be the 'Wow' factor of the whole house, when a prospective female purchaser walks in certainly there will be a noticeable reaction.

This room has to be right, it is often seen as the heart of the house, get it right and it clinches the sale, get it wrong and it makes the rest of the property look below par.

Before I go into more detail about kitchens, the following bits are an absolute must :

It should be absolutely spotlessly clean

There should be uncluttered work surfaces

All pots plates etc put away

The sink and taps should be polished up to shine

It should smell clean, perhaps with a hint of fresh coffee in the pot!

Making your kitchen look fabulous

If after you have cleaned and scrubbed and tidied up you kitchen it still lacks any hint of 'Wow' factor these are the ways to put it right.

Go and look at what is currently 'en vogue' look in the designer kitchen shops and in the magazines. There are many ideas you can borrow to spice up your kitchen.

Obvious quick fixes are to replace the door and drawer handles with newer ones (bought in bulk packs, this is relatively inexpensive)

The door and drawer fronts can be easily painted, or replaced if necessary. Worktops usually take the brunt of the daily wear and tear in a kitchen, and can be replaced with relative ease, and even altered slightly to add a breakfast bar or extra work space. This would also be the time to replace your sink and taps with something more modern.

The kitchen floor can be revamped simply with some modern cushion floor, or laminate, or tiles.

If your wall tiles are dated, again they can be painted, or simply tiled over with a more modern style, and if you replace the old socket fronts with shiny chrome ones it transforms the whole age of the kitchen.

A focal point of a stainless steel cooker hood can make an older kitchen look much younger, and may only cost a few hundred pounds.

The rest of your walls and ceiling can be repainted with some complimentary colour to add a touch of warmth and class, plus covering up all those splashes from years of cooking.

If some of your appliances are at the end of their working life, consider carefully any replacements. Can the new ones be a different colour to enhance the kitchen, or can you go for integrated appliances to make your kitchen look more streamlined.

If your kitchen is small, can it be made to look bigger…..

Go for lighter colours, possibly white unit doors.

Remove some cabinets from one wall.

Move a fridge freezer to a different position to free up space

If there is a dining area, try moving the table, or getting a smaller one.

Take away all items on the work tops except a few select pieces of kitchen ware, like a shiny kettle, a set of ornate storage jars, and a bottle of champagne, and some fresh flowers.

Kitchen Lighting

The room is a show piece so lighting should be bright and reflect off all the shiny surfaces, taps and appliances etc.

Also as it is a room where a lot of work will be going on preparing food so good lighting is essential.

Under cabinet lighting can be used for this illumination, but some recessed spot lights in the ceiling, or a modern central set of spots that can be focussed on certain parts of the kitchen to show it off are great ways to sell the dream.

One Final Note

I know I keep going on about cleaning and polishing, but as there is so much chrome, and other shiny surfaces in a kitchen, if it is dirty, or just not polished up it is easily spotted.

Please use a damp cloth and finally dry cloth to clean and polish all the surfaces, so you can see your face in them, it makes such a difference, just like new.

Conservatory

If you have one it should be a place for relaxation, and to enjoy your garden. Ideally it should have the bear minimum of furniture, a small sofa or two chairs and a coffee table with two or three 'Ideal home' or 'Country Life' magazines on it. There should be room to walk through to the garden and an excellent specimen of a green plant in one corner will finish it off.

Conservatories need a good clean inside and out until the glass sparkles, and if it is winter make sure some form of heating is at the ready, even if it is a £20 convector heater, this can do the trick.

Bathrooms

Similar rules apply as mentioned in the Kitchen section. The bathroom is another chance to woo a prospective purchaser and 'Wow' them into buying your property.

A bathroom is normally the smallest room in the property, but it should be regarded as the one room to relax and rejuvenate you.

Firstly colour, modern trends allow only for a WHITE bathroom suite. You may get away with some pale pastel shade from 'yesteryear' but if you can change the suite to white, and re-tile to a modern taste.

Bathrooms seem to date faster than any room in the house, so change is usually necessary.

You need to create a room of opulence, splendour and relaxation.

Taking note of the displays in the designer showrooms, allow your imagination to create the ideal bathroom.

Light coloured shiny tiles floor to ceiling, white suite, shiny chrome taps. The room should not be cluttered with anything other than new fluffy red or cream towels, new soap, and fancy containers for shampoo etc.

The rest of the clutter should be hidden away in the modern bathroom cabinet or in some cleverly designed fitted bathroom cupboards that add to the modern effect of this relaxing room.

The floor should be tiled, or cushion floor. Wooden laminates are only to be used where they are designed for a bathroom, normal laminates will warp with the moisture.

Depending on the space, a bath with shower overhead, or bath with mixer tap are ideal. But if there is space a separate shower cubical is preferable. When buying a shower look for a cubical that is a reasonable size for the room it is going in. The smallest cubicals available don't allow much room, so try stepping inside a cubical and closing the door behind you before choosing the one for you.

A chrome heated towel rail is very fashionable, but if it is a large bathroom additional heating may be required as well. Matching chrome accessories, toilet roll holder, soap holder etc add a touch of class.

Spotlights in the ceiling help to make all the shiny surfaces shine. More specialised spotlights are used in a bathroom for electrical safety.

The only electrical socket allowed in a bathroom is a shaver socket, and this can be changed to a 'chrome finished' one to add that modern touch.

Mirrors help to make any small room look bigger, and here in a bathroom you can get away with large full-length mirrors, reflecting light around.

Now when you have a bath it is a total experience, and you don't want to get out, lying there with some relaxing music and a glass of wine can be the perfect ending to even the worst day at work !

En-Suites

If you have an en-suite because they are usually so small, it does not take much to re-vamp them if necessary. Mirrors, light colours, opulence, new towels, and no clutter are the main factors. Sometimes just spending a bit of money on a new bathroom cabinet can make an en-suite look fabulous.

Bedrooms

Bedrooms need to be restful, neat and tidy.

We start with the master bedroom, which is normally the biggest and the best.

The focal point of any bedroom is normally the bed, so now is your chance to make it look fantastic, a properly made bed with some element of luxury and comfort in a throw over or new duvet cover to give a touch of class.

Light pastel shades work best in a bedroom as wall colours.

Make sure all clutter is packed away and after the bed, the bedside cabinets and any other furniture add to the luxury and restfulness of the room. Matching bedside lights and soft coloured cushions on the bed.

Any furniture that is rather dated, or looks odd should be removed, failing that repainting built-in wardrobes in a modern pastel shade can transform a bedroom.

Warmth is important in a bedroom so rich thick carpets, or some thick rugs on a bare wooden floor give this effect.

Bedroom windows often look forgotten about, here material in matching colours to the room can add life to the windows, and blinds can be a practical alternative.

All the other bedrooms in the house need the same treatment, and it takes some effort to get them all up to scratch.

Remember the main points in any bedroom are...

Make the bed the focal point of luxury, it should look immaculate and inviting

Paint the wall and ceiling in light restful shades.

De-clutter all surfaces.

Add one or two pieces to 'dress' the room, like flowers or an ornament.

All bedrooms should look like bedrooms and have a bed in them.

If you house is described as a three bedroom house it should have three rooms with a bed in each one. Don't leave any room as a junk room or leave it looking unloved and forgotten about.

Office/Study

Try and have some room in your home as an office/study space, even if you don't use it as such. Many people work from home, or do more work at home than they use to, so just putting a small table and chair with a laptop in the corner of a bedroom, or filling that odd space under the stairs may do the trick.

Unless you have a large property, or an obviously tiny room, don't loose a bedroom and use it as an office instead. A bedroom is always more of a selling point before office space.

Loft Space/Room

If you have a proper room in the loft with proper stairs and the appropriate planning permission it can be described as an extra 'room' or 'bedroom'. If you just have loft ladders, and little else it is really just storage space.

It may be worth applying for planning permission if you have a large loft, and it is something other properties in the neighbourhood have done.

A cheap solution to 'add value' is to board the loft space you have, after making sure you have adequate loft insulation, and putting a strip light up there to give it plenty of light, and painting any bare walls white.

Then for the sake of a few hundred pounds you have masses of storage space, and you can store up here all the bits you have de-cluttered from the rest of the property.

It also shows off the space up there, making your property look bigger and offering more potential to a prospective purchaser.

Back Garden

Your back garden should look well cared for, any lawn should be neatly cut, and all the edges trimmed!

Outside space can add so much to a property. Patio furniture, a table and two or four chairs on the patio give a great look to the garden.

If you have some flags make sure they are clean, if you have the time some simple decking make even the smallest space look appealing.

For a quick DIY job, some anti-weed material and loose light coloured stones can do wonders.

Further down the garden a garden shed, and a small bench to sit on add to the experience. A bird table, and or bird bath add further interest but at little expense.

If you fencing is tatty or damaged, replacing the odd fencing panel, and a coat of fencing paint makes them look like new.

Colour in a garden and no weeds is what you are aiming for, so hard work and some modest expenditure at the garden centre may be needed, but after a day or two great transformations can take place.

If you have a large garden shed come summerhouse it should be shown as a summer house and set out as such.

Garages

Make sure you garage door(s) are freshly painted, and they open easily.

Now is the time to tidy up the garage, throw out or sell all that stuff you will never use.

If you have paint left over giving the inside of a dark and depressing garage a coat of paint makes it look like another useable room!

Try and store everything away neatly on shelves or in cupboards. You want the inside of the garage to look as big as possible.

If the concrete floor of the garage is badly marked or grotty, consider a coat of grey or red concrete floor paint.

Remember

This chapter does give you a lot to do, but once you get started it is amazing how quickly some of these jobs can be done. Half the battle is starting the job.

Time and cost are also a great consideration to all the work that can be done to improve your home, so you can just pick out certain jobs that you feel will have the greatest benefit.

Please don't try and do too many jobs at once, do a list, and try and do one job at once, and when that is completed move on to the next job. It gets very daunting and overwhelming if you try and do too much at once.

Andrew Dale

Chapter 5

A Special Note on Apartments (Flats!)

Apartments need a special chapter to themselves, partly due to the vast amount there seems to be for sale, and also therefore more things you have to do to get yours SOLD.

You own the apartment but the communal parts of the building, and gardens are usually looked after from the maintenance charge that you pay monthly. This also covers interior and exterior painting and roof repairs.

If your building maintenance program has been run properly, or your building is relatively modern, then there may not be much needed to make your building and apartment looking very appealing.

If your apartment is in an older block, then you may have to do some work to sell your property. Usually there will be a maintenance company you contact about the work that needs doing, or a residents committee that discusses any work that needs doing.

Unless you have been in touch with what's going on, and the final phase of some repairs or redecoration is due, then it can take many months, even years to get the jobs done, because so many people have to agree and the money allocated, or found from the residents, and this can be a long process.

So if you are trying to sell an apartment, and you have made sure the inside is immaculate, as discussed in the previous chapter, it is YOU who has to sort out the rest of the building.

I know it does not seem fair that you alone have to keep the building tidy and so on, when perhaps the owners of the other twenty apartments don't seem to care.

But remember it is not for ever it is just to get your apartment sold!

So look at the front garden, and area up to the entrance of the block, if the gardens look a mess then spending a bit of time tidying them up is worth it, even buying a few plants is a good idea, and removing any rubbish from around the property, black bin backs always seem to get left on fire escapes and next to rubbish areas, instead of being moved, this again is down to you.

Inside, if someone walked into your communal hallway does it look appealing ?

Give it a good clean, if the décor is a bit dated, then what is to stop you from giving it a quick coat of emulsion, (You should just mention it to some of the other residents first, but if it's a reasonable colour and you make the place look better they will all be pleased)

If the communal walls look bare or just badly marked in some places then put up one or two pictures to 'lift' the place up.

Then we have to check the 'elevator' or lift, try and keep this clean and smelling pleasant.

Then as you approach the door to your apartment clean walls in the communal hallway, and an impressive looking plant can make a good impression.

If you feel a bit 'silly' doing all this, and think that the other occupants in the building will think you are slightly 'mad', don't worry.

Yes you can go and pick the rubbish up, and move the bin bags when other people are out at work if you feel better doing it then, but most people will appreciate you trying to keep their building looking good.

If anyone does confront you about the jobs you are doing, which is pretty unlikely, all you have to say is that you had some emulsion paint left over from painting your apartment, and you thought you would use it up. Or if you are doing the garden, then you just thought you would get a bit of exercise in the fresh air. You may be annoyed that no-one else is helping, but don't say it. You need to try and keep everyone happy, the last thing you need when you are trying to sell your apartment is a major disagreement with any of the other residents.

So keep on top of making your apartment block clean and tidy, and remove any junk mail or free papers that seem to get delivered almost daily.

Again double check communal areas when a viewing is imminent, you never know when yet another black bag of rubbish can mysteriously appear.

The front door of your block should create a good impression, so paint it if necessary and polish up any brass door furniture !

Another thing that apartment blocks seem to attract is their fair share of 'abandoned' cars and other unwanted items – get them moved, your local council will collect a maximum of three household items at a time, without any charge, but you may have to wait a week or two so ring them now, and get it booked in !

Abandoned cars that are NOT on a public highway, or council land can be a problem, so check that the car does not belong to anyone else in the building, you can put a sign on the vehicle, stating that it should be removed by the owner within fourteen days, and the date, and that if it is not removed, then it will be towed away.

If you can't get any joy, then a scrap yard will collect it, sometimes free, sometimes for a small fee, also speak to any small local one man band garages where they do repairs etc, they will help, or know someone who can.

There is nothing worse than having an abandoned car not only taking up a much needed car parking space, but gradually looking worse and worse week by week, and being vandalised right outside the front door of the very impressive apartment you are offering for sale!

The other point is to make your property sound a bit more saleable, for instance if your block is called 'Oakwood' or 'Norbreck House' there is nothing to stop you from calling it 'Oakwood Apartments', or 'Norbreck Mansions', and if you don't have a sign at the entrance, or it has seen better days, than why not get a new sign done to add a bit of value to your property.

When you do your sales pack of the plus points of the apartment you should put down the maintenance charge you pay and if it is paid monthly and what is included in that i.e buildings insurance, garden maintenance, cleaning etc, because anyone who has not owned an apartment before would not understand what it is for. The other items you could list is all the improvements that have been made & work done within the last few years, and any jobs lined up to be done in the near future.

This shows the property is being looked after and is a good investment, and overcome any doubts that are lurking in their minds.

Another point regarding apartments is the fact that for someone who does not want the hassle of a garden, or to have jobs to do around their home, it is a bonus.

Security wise most people, especially women and older people feel, and usually rightly so much safer living alone in an apartment than they would in a house on their own.

Just knowing there is someone else in the building you could shout out to, or a neighbours door you could knock on quickly in case of emergency.

Also in terms of burglary etc most apartment blocks are more secure than the average house.

Also an apartment on the second floor or above can have some amazing views that you would never get in a house.

Affordability, more affordable than a house, also bigger rooms and more space than you may get for the same amount of money spent on a house.

So apartments do have an awful lot going for them.

The downside has recently been over supply, because for developers the most profitable way to make money was to put a block of apartments on the land, so everyone and their brother was doing it.

Then with the 'buy to let' market going into overdrive the actual price of some of these apartments was unrealistically high. Now the market is slower financial institutions want a larger deposit on new build apartments as greater security, and to be sure the price of the apartments is realistic.

So if you have an older apartment you are trying to sell this could certainly be used in your favour, but if it is a new build apartment you are selling just make sure you concentrate on marketing it at a very realistic price.

Chapter 6

Finding the Best Estate Agent

Estate Agents have had a very bad press in the past, this has partly been due to a few bad apples spoiling the reputation for the rest of the Profession.

It is not a mandatory requirement to have any qualifications to be an Estate Agent, and with the large sums of money involved it can be open to some malpractice.

The business they are in is not as easy one, and we as the customer tend to automatically blame the agent when things go wrong. It is very much a 'People' business and the whole process of interaction between 'buyer' and 'seller' needs to be handled very carefully.

I have dealt with many Estate Agents in the past and found them to be very professional in their own way, but like any type of profession some people are better suited to it than others, what you are looking for are the best!

Check for agents that have one or more of the following sets of letters after their names……

ANAEA   Associate of the National Association of Estate Agents

ARICS   Associate of the Royal Institute Of Chartered Surveyors

ASVA   Associate of the Society of Valuers and Auctioneers

Choosing the right estate agent or agents is crucial to the sale of your property, yes, you can try and sell your property on your own, but in my experience choosing the right Estate Agent can give your property exposure to the greatest number of potential buyers in the shortest space of time, and help to secure a sale. It also gives your property, and the asking price far greater credibility.

In 'boom' times anybody can sell a property relatively easily, but in harder times when there are fewer buyers, and more properties 'for sale' you need the best help you can get, and as much of it as possible.

The Estate Agent is not some magician who can magically sell your house on their own, you need to think of them as Professionals who you can work with, and it is a joint venture, a joint effort, they are doing their best to market and get people to view, and you are doing your best to sell the property when people come round.

So you need to select an agent, or agents you feel a rapport with, and can work along side.

How to Choose an Estate Agent

To select an agent firstly make a list of all the agents in your area from the local telephone book, yellow pages, local newspaper and from internet listing for your area.

Look at the Estate Agents boards in your area, and more importantly the ones with **'Sale Agreed'** and **'Sold'** on them.

Ask for recommendations from friends, relatives, and work colleagues for Estate Agents they have used in the past and been happy with.

At this point you are just doing a reconnaissance mission to find possible agents to come and look at your property.

Visit each agents offices, firstly on a weekday and then secondly at weekend.

(Note the weekend staff can differ from the weekly staff)

See how their offices are laid out, and if they are selling properties, particularly ones similar to yours. Putting your two bed apartment with an agent who specialises mainly in country houses is not going to help.

Notice how busy the office is or not, and how friendly the staff are, do they greet you with a smile and show interest?

Look at the properties similar to yours, and particularly the details and photographs.

Do they look appealing, are the photographs on display large and bright, and showing the properties in a good light?

You'll be amazed how some agents have poor, dark, badly taken photos.

Collect the details of at least one or two properties similar to yours from each agent you visit. Sometimes an agent will have a sales list of properties, or a glossy magazine, collect that as well for reference.

Some agents have sales details already on display for you to take as many as you wish, some will have display boards, and you will have to ask for further details to take away on each property.

You are also waiting to see what reaction you get from the Estate Agency staff, you will normally be asked if you need help, if you respond by saying 'just looking', and see if they respond any further, (a good agent will ask what type of property you are looking for), then you can mention you are thinking of selling your property soon, and you are looking at what's available, but if the office is busy don't take up much of their time just now.

It is a good opportunity to stand and look around the property displayed and at the same time listen in to conversations going on, either on the phone with other customers, and between the agency staff themselves. A lot can be learned from the activities like this……..are they professional, discussing sales and working hard to help people, you don't want anyone sat there doing nothing, or going into great detail about their night out, it's simply not professional, especially when you are on the premises !

As soon as you step out of one office make a note on the sales leaflets of the responses you got from the staff, and do this before you visit the next agent, otherwise you will forget. Write down the names of the people you have spoken to, and taken special note of who seems to be the most enthusiastic and helpful person in the office.

Visit all the agents in your area, this can take some time, it could easily be 15 or more, then I suggest you go to the nearest tea shop and have a rest and a cup of tea!

Now what you need to do is narrow it down to about five agents, and this is the main criteria for choosing…..

You want the Estate Agents that are…..

- ✓ Friendly, helpful and professional, preferably in a busy office

- ✓ Selling property similar to yours

- ✓ Displaying a large amount of 'Sold' and 'Sale Agreed' properties

- ✓ Using high quality property sales details with descriptions that make you want to buy every property, accompanied by good photographs and floor plans

- ✓ In a prominent location with good window displays

- ✓ Open long hours, seven days a week!

Floor Plans

Floor plans are a great selling point showing how all the rooms in a property are laid-out, this allows a purchaser to see at a glance the number of rooms and whether it will suit their requirements or not. This can save wasting time for both parties, and are probably one of the best selling tools, given how important this is, I am surprised all Estate Agents don't use them, but if your Estate Agent does it is a definite advantage over the others.

Property Details

Some agents will have just one A4 sheet, and just one photograph, others have an A3 sheet folded to A4 size with six or seven photographs. The descriptive words from one agent to another vary, some are more daring than others, but you need excellent descriptions that can convey the quality and uniqueness of a property. You will be surprised how a little effort and imaginative wording can make you want to go and see a property. We will spend more time on this subject later on page...., but for now lets get back to business......

When you have narrowed it down to about five agents, visit them again on a Saturday or Sunday, and see how the weekend staff respond to you.

If all these agents give you a good positive greeting then fine, but if only three or four then narrow it down to those few.

Go Online

The next step is to go on the internet and check out the properties these final selected Estate Agents are advertising. The agents details will probably have the web sites, but just in case, the most popular are listed at the back of this book.

Check out the properties you have found by the finally selected agents.

Check the listings for details and how they stand out, pictures and words.

Have they all past the final test?

Anyway, you really want to end up with a minimum of THREE estate agents coming to see your property, but definitely no more than FIVE.

Getting the Estate Agents to view you property

As covered in a previous chapter your property should be immaculate, even before the agent comes around !

Make sure it is properly presented just like a show house, ready for a prospective purchaser to come round.

Try and book all the agents on the **same day**, this means you contacting them at least one or two weeks in advance and juggling times and dates around, write down the possible days and times first, and then you will have to ring them back once or twice until it all works out on the same day.

This is going to be a very busy day, first to get everything just perfect and then to get each agent one after the other, try and get them at hourly intervals, as some agents may be late or early for their appointment.

When The Estate Agent Arrives

The person who visits from the agency is normally a sales person whose sole job is to visit prospective clients, sometimes it is the main person i.e. the owner of the business or Director, if it is part of a chain of agents it may be the branch manager/manageress.

This is what they normally do, all day long, five days a week... they drive (probably in a BMW) with a folder, and they look at your property, do a short sales presentation to you about their company, congratulate you on your great property and say what they think it is worth and how they will sell it.

This person is out and about to get business in for the company.

This person is not normally the person in the office whose job it is to sell your property.

A good agent should have done some research before they arrive, they should have a few details of similar properties, and have also checked property that has recently sold in your area, and obtained the actual selling prices achieved off the various websites, not just the 'For Sale' prices.

(note: you can do this yourself…….check the internet, and with the homework you have already done you will have a good idea of what your property may be worth, but don't tell the Estate Agent this, not just yet anyway!)

Showing the agent around

Show the agent around first, point out exactly what is included as part of the property ie, boundaries of your garden, sometimes the amount of land is not apparent, especially with country houses, also with apartments, some have their own private garden, when at first glance an agent may just assume it is communal space. This can make a big difference to the price and saleability of a property.

You don't need to go into every detail of your family history at the same time!

This is business so get the points across. It is best to make a list before the agent comes about what the property offers and give a copy to the agent after going through it with them.

Have your pen and paper at the ready for notes...

Here are the questions to ask each agent.....

1) Price for your property   Highest Price ?
   Lowest Price ?

2) State of the market at the moment ?

3) What have you sold recently?

4) What is your fee, is it 'no sale no fee' and are there any additional charges?

5) Do you do joint agencies, and what is your fee for this, and what other agencies do you work well with ?

6) What do you provide with the internet and virtual tours?

7) How saleable is this type of property?

8) What other services do you offer, are they part of the service or at extra cost? i.e. accompanied viewings etc.

9) What other things do you think I can do to sell this property in terms of presentation, please tell me honestly what you would do if it was your property?

10) Timescale for selling?

Don't automatically choose the agent who is going to charge you the lowest commission, or the agent who values your property at the highest price. What you want is to sell it quickly and easily !

More than one agent

One point to make here is the prospect of having more than one agent acting for you, and I would recommend having two agents.

You can have two (or even more) agents acting for you, choosing two different types of agent one can be a rather pushy agent, and the other older more established and perhaps better known.

The idea is that you can have the best of both worlds, two are better than one as the saying goes!

Yes, you will pay slightly more commission, but it may be only slightly more, some agents work on a one third two third split….

The agent who sells the property, not necessarily the introducing agent !, ie if one introduces the property to the client, but the purchaser then decides to put the offer in with the other agent, simply because their office was nearer to where they live, and that agent then follows up and the sale goes through, then that agent is then the selling agent.

The process would be finalised when your solicitor pays them the FULL commission, and then they would pay one third to the other agent. As long as both agents are made aware in the first place they are joint agents, then there should not really be a problem.

Some agents are pushy, too pushy, and although they may introduce a property to a client, because there is so much at stake, and people get very stressed out even looking at property, sometimes the slightest thing like a pushy, over bearing agent, or a mixed up appointment time is more than enough for a prospective purchaser to say 'forget it' or some other more graphic phrase, and they will not go back to that agent even if they are handling the sale of what may be the perfect home for them.

To clarify the options...

Sole Agency	You put your property in the hands of one agent only. You pay about 1.5% commission or less, and they sell it !
Joint Sole Agency	You put your property with two agents who work together, but in competition to sell it. You may pay a bit more, but not always. The commission is split two thirds, and one third, or twenty five percent and seventy five percent.

Multi Agency   You can have as many agents as you want, but the one that sells gets a higher commission, usually 2% or higher.

You can now narrow it down to the best Agent or the best two agents if you wish, and clarify the commission, I would recommend NOT trying to beat them down on commission, just ask for their best deal, and leave it at that. What you want is the property sold, if your property is going to earn them the lowest commission it is not much of an incentive for them to sell it!

Invite them back to your property to fill in the paperwork and sort out the photographs.

Photographs

You have chosen the best agent(s) partly because the photographs were good, and you want to ask for the photographs to be taken on a sunny day of the exterior.

If you are a budding amateur photographer, or you know someone who is into photography, what you need is primarily photos taken with a very wide angle lens to show on paper the whole of each room or main rooms. This is not as easy as it sounds, when we look at a room our eyes and brain automatically scan the room, but a camera will only photograph what the lens can see.

Technically the equipment that is ideal is a digital SLR camera with a wide angle lens ideally 10mm (or 17mm for a full frame digital SLR). Yes, I know this sounds a bit technical, but I have photographed property myself, and believe me trying to photograph a kitchen, bathroom, or an en-suite can be very difficult to convey all that is in that room.

To get the angle of view of the room, try from various angles, it is not always the obvious angle that looks the best. I have taken doors off the hinges to get more of the room in, and to not have part of the door in the picture. Even go outside and try taking the photos through an OPEN window of the room inside.

But when you are taking exterior photographs make sure all the windows are closed, and all curtains, blinds etc are drawn back neatly.

One set of six to ten photographs is the normal requirement. The main image of the exterior is the most important, but be careful here, it may be that the back of your house looks like a mansion, and the front looks like a normal house, so use the back of the house as your main photograph to grab the attention of a prospective purchaser.

Similarly, if you are trying to sell 'a not to special' property, but it has an amazing view from any of its windows, then use that view instead as the main photo.

This is to illustrate that it does not necessarily have to be a square on shot of the front of your house. But if that is what you go for here are some tips…..

All your photographs need to be 'landscape' format, that means holding the camera in it's normal position, and not having it on it's side, this is due to the fact your photographs are going to be on websites, and match the format of a computer screen.

Make sure it is a bright day with blue sky, wait for the sun to be in the best position, normally behind the photographer.

Now if you have four cars & a caravan & boat & three kids bicycles in the front garden……move them out the way for the photographs!

What you want is a clear image of the property, but if you have an amazing front garden try and get some of that in, and if you have a nice car, a red sports car, a BMW, Mercedes etc having that strategically placed to be captured can help to show your property as something special, and something to be aspired to.

I know someone who used to get his friend to park his Rolls Royce outside a house every time he was ready to put it up for sale, just so it looked better on the agents photographs, and it did help……..how many estate agents photographs normally have a Rolls Royce on them?

The point is to get the photos right, by all means your agents photos may be excellent but if you are not happy with them, having them done by yourself, or someone else is a way of making your property stand out from the rest.

An agent or their own photographer will not spend as much time on the photos, i.e. 20 minutes may be your lot (after all he has another three properties to photograph before lunch and another four after that)

However, if you do them yourself you can wait until the weather and sunlight is right on the front of the property for that photo, then wait until it is right on your back garden , perhaps in the afternoon for that photo, and you can move furniture and accessories around in the rooms, turn lights on and off etc. to see which gives the most pleasing images.

Yes, it can be a lot of messing but it will be well worth it. When I have done this it has taken an hour or two, but it has been great fun, take as many photographs at different angles and hold the camera at different heights, ideally put it on a tripod and have the tripod about three to four feet high, this gives a good guide for a room shot.

If your agent does not want any images from anyone other than them, for any LEGAL reason, then explain that you want to sell the property !

If all else fails...

What I have done in the past is when someone has been to view, I have given them my photos myself, or one or two A4 photocopied sheets with them on, we will cover this in the chapter on viewings.

Right, you have chosen the agent(s) photos done, the works.

Now you want to ask for the following:-

1. You want a 'Special' in the local paper, some call it a 'Feature', or 'Agents View', or 'Property Of The Week', but it is a sales tool to get people to notice your property. This is part of their service, but there may be a waiting list……
I have found that if you ask politely your property can normally be given priority as a special case, and appear within a few weeks.

2. You want your property to be in the local paper, and on the internet ASAP, and you want a good position in the agents window display, (ideally head height, about 5 ft 6 inches from the ground, and in the main 'HOT SPOT' part of the window)

3. You want the people in the office, the people who are actually sat there trying to sell your property, to come and see it, not too much to ask is it? Ideally you will be assigned to a certain person on the sales team, responsible for 'selling' your property so get them along, again everything to be immaculate. Then also get one of the weekend staff along. The more office staff

that see your property the better, and make them remember you by offering them a cup of tea and slice of cake!

This need not take too long just be nice, show them around all the property point out the selling points and shake their hand, and tell them you want it sold.

This is a major plus point, how often have you been to an agent and asked about a property, and no-one in the office has actually seen it?

Imagine going into buy a washing machine and you ask the salesman about it, and he obviously knows nothing about the product, are you impressed, do you buy the product ? – exactly.

But it happens with property, so insist that a 'Monday to Friday' person and a 'Saturday & Sunday' person come out as a matter of urgency.

The agents main selling tools are....

1 Internet

2 'For Sale' board

3   Office sales details, window display, inside display, sales particulars

4   Newspaper advertising

5   Staff knowledge & customer service & selling skills

6   Lists of prospective customer requirements – Mailing lists, Texts, email

Not necessarily in that order, but most is related to the internet and electronic communication these days.

The majority of initial enquiries are generated by the internet, even your grandma looking for her retirement apartment may spend more time 'silver surfing' than looking in her local newspaper.

Very Important

Your agent will send you a 'draft copy' of your sales details, please READ them properly at least two or three times, if it does not sound right or something has been missed, scribble down what corrections you want, and send it back, this you can do as many times as you want until you are happy with it. Some agents now are very cautions as to what they put down on paper, under the misrepresentation act designed to stop them saying something that is not true. How some agents interpret this varies quite a lot.

For instance what do you call 'Large', has your property got a large lounge, if you went to Buckingham Palace, does her majesty also have a large lounge, but possible it may be larger than yours !

You see it's difficult to draw the line, a friend of ours was chatting with a couple at a garden centre, the other couple were explaining they had a large garden and wanted to have a water feature installed, our friends had just had one installed in their back garden and were about to extol the virtues of the one they had purchased for a mere £ 250, but wisely before stepping in they asked how large the couples garden was, "well" the couple quietly replied, "Its about two acres, and then there's about an acre of woodland"

Enough rambling……

Check your details also on the internet, are the photographs correct etc.

Check the details in the agents office.

List of USP's in the agents' details?

I cannot stress enough how important it is for you to check, and double check all the ways your property is being marketed, you know your property much better than the agent, if they make a mistake, it is up to you to spot it.

After a week, pop in to the agents to check all is up to speed.

Agents know that the first few days and weeks are crucial for both them and you, and the prospect of a sale.

They will focus on your property as soon as it is ready to go. They will try and get viewings, to show you they are doing their job, and to push, push, push, this 'amazing new property' that has only just hit the market and must not be missed !

Chapter 7

Setting The Right Price

As we have mentioned price…..

You need to be very realistic in a slow market as to the price you put your property on the market for, and also the price you see as the lowest price you will accept.

Rarely these days does someone come along and say yes I'll pay the purchase price, as they may have done a few years ago!

The more usual way is for them to put an offer in quite a bit lower than you have on the Estate Agents details.

Depending on local conditions, and how desperate you are let's illustrate the point….

Originally you thought your house was worth £ 225,000, now in slow times you think £ 200,000 would be good. Well, I would advise a marketing price of £ 199,950 No Chain Delay ! and see what happens, any offer of £ 180,000 or more should seriously be considered, especially from a buyer who is not in a CHAIN.

Bear in mind the Stamp duty thresholds, and price your property accordingly, and allow to take at least 5-10 % less than the price on your agents details.

Only accept an offer on the assurance that a surveyor will call around fairly quickly and that a sale can be completed within a set period of time.

Chapter 8

Incentives

These can be seen as 'bribes', but they are perfectly legal and really are no more than sales tools and if you like 'gimmicks', designed to get your property noticed and SOLD.

Incentives to get people to come and view your property..

Have an Open day !

You advertise an open day for the viewing of your property and along with your agent you try and get as many people to view, say between the hours of 10am and 3pm.

The plus point is you can have your property set up ready well in advance, and just having different potential purchasers viewing when other are there, this can give a sense of competition between them. You can have some proper presentation packs ready to hand out and a glass of wine or cup of tea for each viewer. Just try and get other members of your family or a person from the Estate Agents to help you out on the day, just in case all the viewers turn up at once!

This is not just people going to look at a property but also a bit of a social get together, it breaks the ice and can be very successful.

Hopefully the weather will be kind to you!

Also you could advertise, FREE glass of wine for every viewer, or free bottle of wine, or buffet etc.

All these types of sales gimmicks have been tried and tested in the past and can get people through your door.

Incentives for them to buy your property.......

Price your property correctly

Stamp duty paid

Deposit paid

Solicitors fees paid

Six or twelve months mortgage paid

Include Furniture, carpets, curtains, washing machine, fridge freezer etc – ready to move in to.

No Chain delay!

Look at all the incentives the big house builders do to get people to buy their properties, then use some of their ideas !

Chapter 9

No Chain

This subject deserves a little chapter all to itself simply because it is the single most beneficial position both for you as a seller and any prospective purchaser.

The two immortal words 'No Chain' can take away such a lot of messy situations.

The advantage for the purchaser is that you are NOT going to be as likely to delay or let them down at some later stage in the process due to the fact your sale is dependant on multiple sets of other people moving at the same time.

To give your property probably the most beneficial USP you yourself should not be in a chain.

So have your house up for sale, have next to the price of your property on the agents details... NO Chain Delay.

Then when you have viewers come round extol the virtues of your No

Chain Situation.

You can move at a moments notice, you will move to suit the person who purchases your property, you are the ideal seller.

The whole buying/selling process is fraught with enough problems, you reduce the chances of a sale falling through or being delayed by cutting out the number of factors your sale depends on.

So please, please, please, to sell your property 'No Chain' is the way forward.

You can go in a B & B.

Some smaller B&B's will give you an excellent rate if you explain the situation and want to stay with them for a month at a time.

You can stay with relatives or work colleagues

You can just rent a small flat or house

Can you pay someone £ 80.00 a week on the 'rent-a-room scheme'

Has someone you know got a holiday cottage or caravan you could rent for a short time.

Some holiday parks rent out chalets and caravans virtually all year round, and if you research carefully it is surprising how little some of them charge, you may have to move from one park to another after a few weeks to comply with the rules and regulations, but it can be great fun, and a bit of a holiday that you really deserve after selling your property !

You can purchase a second-hand holiday caravan on a site within a matter of days for under £ 10,000 in some parts of this country (bear in mind you can only stay in them for seven to ten months of the year) but these can be an ideal solution if you run out of a place to move to quickly.

Holiday flats can be rented quickly if necessary, you can usually get a reduced rate if you are staying there for matter of months rather than weeks, and particularly if it is out of the normal holiday season.

The problems that you can face are....

What do we do with the furniture ? well, unless it has great sentimental value you have various options, leave it in your property as a gift to the purchasers, or allow them to buy it at very reasonable prices.

Put it into storage, companies charge £ 20.00 a week to store a reasonable amount of your prized furniture.

Sell it, donate it or give it away.

The main thing is to sell your house, in the scale of things I don't understand why people insist on trailing washing machines, fridge-freezers, and old wardrobes around as though they are some prized possession. Normally they may amount to only a few hundred pounds at best, and the costs of getting a removal company to move them can be quite high.

So don't risk jeopardising the sale of your property, just because you won't move quickly because you want to cling on to a few items of furniture, or you find somewhere suitable to have them move with you. This may be just the time to start a fresh when you get settled into your next home.

You may have to travel a bit further to work…yes, but it's surely worth it not to be worrying about your property selling or not, and it can make life a bit more interesting.

If you have children they can adapt remarkably well to temporary accommodation, sometime much more so than we do!

The next stage of NO Chain is…….

Yes, you want a purchaser who is also not in a chain….

So ask your estate agent to check their books, and to seek out any viewers in this enviable position.

So once again can I stress to you the mantra of:-

No Chain, No Chain, No Chain, No Chain……….

Then when it's all done, and you are looking for a new property to buy YOU are in the great position to say that you have nothing to sell, and anyone wanting to sell their property should welcome you with open arms!

Chapter 10

Mortgages

"At one time, anyone with a pulse was a good candidate for a mortgage"

I heard this saying recently from a financial adviser, describing how things use to be…….in the good times !

I know myself that when I was buying a property, providing I had a reasonable deposit and a reasonably good credit rating I could buy anything within reason.

Now things are very different, financial institutions are not so eager to lend money. You really need to have a large deposit, a good credit rating (never to have missed any mortgage payment ever!) a good job, and then they may consider you.

Not easy !!

Financial institutions are rightly more cautious and double check all the applications.

There are some exceptions…

But if your prospective purchaser is a Doctor, Accountant, Dentist, Solicitor, or works for the civil service then they are usually a pretty safe bet.

A young person these days may be lucky enough to have parents to 'lend' them the deposit for a property, and also act as 'guarantor' to enable their 'child' to get on the property ladder.

This is becoming more and more common. Trying to give your children a good start in life is a priority with most parents', it just depends on how deep your pockets are.

Remember that old Joke…….

"The wife asks her husband if he can remember the last time their son came back home from university, and the husband replies, just a minute dear I'll have to look in my cheque book for exactly what date that was!!"

Anyway if a young person comes to view your property, don't write them off straight away, they may be a young solicitor, or their parents may have already given their backing to buy a property.

One of my son's friends was helped to buy a house, with his parents very kindly putting down a deposit of £ 100,000.00 !

If you are friendly with a mortgage advisor it may be worthwhile checking exactly what is available for a prospective purchaser, they may be able to offer a little bit more of an insight into a mortgage situation, compared to just a high street bank or building society.

Remember you are not trying to sell a mortgage to the person looking at your property, no-one ever wants a mortgage, we don't get to the age of 18 or twenty and rush out and say I want a mortgage !

What we do say is that we want a place of our own, and the only way to get it (short of a lottery win or great aunty Margorie popping off rather sharpish) is to buy it with a whapping big loan !…….known as a mortgage.

So show someone they can afford the home of their dreams with the right mortgage and you may just have sold it there and then.

If you want more of an idea of this go and see any new developments and ask about what they can do in terms of mortgages !

There are people out there who do not need a mortgage, they have got the cash either from selling their property and down sizing, inheritance or whatever.

A very successful friend of mine, who wrote computer games, just saved up his earnings and paid £ 350,000 cash for his first house !

Chapter 11

The Viewings

When your agent contacts you to arrange a viewing try to be flexible and let people come round at any time within reason, but also try and set the times to your advantage to show your property at its' best.

For example if your property is next to a school, having a viewing at 3.30pm on a weekday afternoon when everyone is trying to collect their kids is not ideal, your prospective viewer may struggle to get near your property, let alone park their car!

Be sure to write down the name & time of the person or persons viewing, and repeat it back to the agent.

Ask about the position of the person viewing, is their house on the market, have they got a sale going through, or are they in rented accommodation?

There is no real point in having viewings with a person who has not even got their home on the market.

People do lie about their position.

Ideally if you are not in a chain, see section NO CHAIN, you want to get someone else who is also not in a chain.

This makes it much easier for both purchaser and vendor, you have no-one else either up or down a chain to mess things up and complicate the issue, all you have to do is sort out the price, moving dates and you are sorted!

Your agent may already have knowledge of your prospective viewers' situation and may have shown them various properties before, and built up a relationship with them, this is better for all concerned, and can save a lot of wasted time.

Your personal safety is paramount when viewing, so if you are a lady on your own, please either get a friend or relative to pop round to your property when you have a viewing, or arrange with the Estate Agent to send someone to accompany you. As well as the safety issue, this also helps with your confidence when meeting someone for the first time.

Show Time

Make sure everything is neat and tidy, a half hour before the viewing is due double check outside, your front garden and particularly from the kerb.

You would be amazed how many bits of rubbish can stick by your gate post, and worse still a little message from a passing dog!

Put lights on in your property, wall lights etc, even if it's daylight, and put your heating on slightly if there is any chill in the air.

Any real fire or attractive lounge fire should be lit as a rule, some fire you can just have the light on without the heat, for show.

Any children or dogs should ideally be packed off to neighbours, or the park, or grannies for an hour or so, until told it is safe to return !

If there is a busy main road outside keep the windows closed to reduce the noise levels, but open the rear door to the garden and rear windows to let fresh air in if it is a lovely warm day.

Don't judge a book by its cover

As your prospective buyers arrive you will normally have spotted them, noted what car they arrive in and how they are dressed, and made an assumption on this in your own mind as to whether you are wasting your time!

Do not be disappointed, either way you can have someone in new BMW's with not a penny to their name, and also someone with a ten year old Volvo estate with enough money in the bank to pay cash for your property, so remember appearances can be deceptive !

Anyway, show time……

Don't be too eager to rush out to them, give them time to get out of their limozine !

Let them admire the front of your property, and take in the palm tree by the front door.

Introduce yourself, and remember their names (you have written them down) and use their names, a persons name is the sweetest sound they can here.

So greet, smile and say 'Hello, Mr & Mrs Jones' easy.

Start obviously in the hallway, then the lounge, and work your way around.

Try to let the viewers go into the room in front of you and you can stay in the hallway, but insight of the viewer, so you can answer questions and point out one or two features in each room, particularly if your property is on the small side.

Don't rush round let them look properly at their own pace. Sometimes they won't waste much time, and know instinctively if it is right for them or not, but surprisingly many viewers are either rather quiet or complementary to your property, and are only too aware it is your home, and they don't want to offend you, even if they don't like it.

Remember your kitchen, if it has integrated appliances, dishwasher, fridge freezer, washing machine, all cleverly hidden behind matching doors it should be you who goes and open them all for your viewers to look, people don't like opening your kitchen cupboards!

This is your chance to show off all the integrated items that will be included in the sale price.

Point out where your Gas & Electric meters are located.

Have a good reason ready for why you are moving from such a perfect place!

After showing them around, ask them if they have any questions....

Answer them properly, clearly, and without rambling on too much.

Ask if they have a copy of the agents sales sheet, unless they have come direct form the agents, chances are they have not got a proper copy of your details, so make sure you have a few spare to hand out to viewers.

Then it's your turn to ask about them…..

Ask about their circumstances, they may tell you much more than they let on to the estate agents….

Where are they up to, have they sold?

Are they living with relatives or renting ?

When do they have to move, have they got any deadline, you are looking for clues as to how you and your situation can help them.

Ideally you are not in a chain, and make the best situation for them…

When can you move ?

Very quickly within a matter of weeks...

Where are you going ?

Staying with relatives, short term let, caravan park, time off work, etc..

Show what a good prospect you are, how flexible, and eager to help them, and in turn this helps you to get what you want... No.1 priority - to sell your property !

Present your details like offering a gift!

Now is the time to hand over your specially printed "sales sheets", this is your answer to all the questions that normally pop up in the mind of a prospective purchaser:-

Council tax band

Local Schools and position in league tables

Bus stops & routes

Local leisure centre & Gyms

Local parks

Maintenance charges (for an apartment)

New Double glazing

New Central heating

South facing rear garden

Provision for car parking, car space

Neighbours

Safe neighbourhood

Peace & quiet

Your USP's in a list

More Photographs if necessary.

The fact that you are not in a chain in writing, and you can move quickly.

It's easy to reel all these off during a viewing, but when they get home and sort through the ten properties they have looked at that day, how are they going to remember all the reasons they should choose yours?

Simply having them laid out in black and white for them to read through as many times as they like when they get home, put the TV on, open that bottle of wine and have another look at all your photographs.

Then finally ask them if they would like to look around again, and if you feel happy you can give them a little bit more room to look by themselves.

(It's common sense, but please, please make sure any valuables, hand bags and wallets etc are not just left out, most people are honest and would not touch them anyway, but it's best just to be a little bit cautious.)

Then at the end of the viewing thank them for coming.....

If you are asked the next few questions........

PRICE?

If you are asked about the price, be polite, and don't get into an argument or debate about what price you will take, it is best to say that they will need to put an offer in to the agents, and leave it at that, or that "obviously I do want to sell my property, please put an offer in to the agents and I am sure we come to an acceptable figure for both of us."

VIEWINGS?

How many viewings have you had, have you had any offers, be careful here, because they may have asked your estate agent the same thing just before they arrived, so don't come up with a big fat lie !

Usually, the best answers are true ..

Well, I have had quite a bit of interest but it has only been on the market two weeks

I have had someone, but they haven't got a buyer for theirs

I have had someone and they are popping back with their husband next week.

TELEPHONE NUMBER?

Lets forget the estate agent, give me your phone number, and we'll sort it out between us !

NO.

If the person is slightly underhand to suggest this tactic, then what is to stop them putting in a much lower offer the day you are about to exchange contracts ? commonly known as GAZUNDERING !

Also, exchanging phone numbers at this early stage is not a good idea, you simply reply that you would be happier if we dealt through the estate agents initially, until the deal has been done, and then later we can exchange phone numbers, just to sort out any bits.

From my experience it is really always best to go through your agent and solicitor, so that there are no misunderstandings. Also despite their poor reputation, you will find in MOST estate agents a person whose job it is to deal with people, and providing they have had enough experience, they can listen to the concerns and ranting and ravings of both sides, and then make sense of it to try and keep both sides happy, and make sure the sale goes through.

So you have been through the viewing, explain that if they want to come back for a second viewing they only need to ask the agent, and likewise any questions...

That's it !

NOW FEEDBACK....

A good agent will contact the person who viewed your property normally a day or two later, to get an idea of what they thought of your property.

This is very important, and you should welcome all the feedback from your agent.

Was it suitable for them

The location

The size

The price

Would they like to put an offer in

What did they like and dislike.

If you have ten people all like the property but won't put an offer in, or they say it seems a bit too expensive, then your price is probably too high, and you are putting people off.

Some viewers will have a list of properties they are looking at over a period of time, and due to their job, and their partners commitments may not be able to view together, and when one of them likes a property and wants to get their partners opinion it could be another week before it can be arranged.

So the point is bear in mind that yours will not be the only property they have seen, and it may take a bit more time than you would like before a person who has viewed actually says yes or no to a second viewing, or writes your property off all together – heaven forbid!

SECOND VIEWINGS

Now, don't be lazy, just because the couple who came last time in the new BMW, have decided to grace you with their presence again, it is not a time to miss cleaning up the 'doggy mess' at the front gate!

Make sure everything is doubly spotless, this could be make or break!

Your property may now be on their short list, so competition could be fierce.

But you don't have to repeat the whole sales 'speel' again – just the vital points.

If they have brought round their partner or other friend or relative, then allow them time to investigate the property.

You need to remain positive.

If you are asked about what you are leaving, usually the carpets and possibly curtains, the best reply is "it depends on the price."

These can be a bargaining tool.

If you get a good offer then you will leave A, B, C, but obviously if you take a rather low offer then you will do a list of items for sale separately with prices along side them.

Make the main points finally, i.e. No Chain and be enthusiastic!

Chapter 12

The Surveyor

When you have accepted an offer on your property the next step is for the surveyor to call and access the property.

These are one of three types, Valuation, Home buyers report, Structural survey.

Other than make sure your property is still looking at it's best there is not much else you can do.

The surveyor will normally ask you the agreed price and one or two other basic questions before walking around your property making notes. The main thing you worry about is if they will accept that the agreed price is reasonable.

They will also take notes on the condition of the property inside and out, for a valuation this is very brief, but for a home buyers report more in depth, a structural survey is not very common for an average property for sale, but could take a few hours to complete.

The surveyor just needs to have confirmed exactly what the boundaries of your property are, and this needs particular notice if you are selling an apartment with any land/garden/parking stipulated as owned by the flat and shown in the lease.

The surveyor is acting for the person buying your property and the lending institution, and does not, and will not normally say much to you about what he is writing down.

You just have to be polite & helpful leave him to do his assessment and then wait until you are notified by you estate agent or solicitor as to the next stage.

The survey may have come up with some questions which you need to answer quickly and as professionally as you can.

The main point is ... Has the surveyor valued it at the agreed price... if he has fine, no matter what else has been put in the survey, which does tend to list a lot of stuff which can sound very off putting but really it is just the surveyor trying to make sure there is no come back on him at some latter stage.

If the surveyor says at the end, yes the price I value this property at is £200,000 and that's what you have agreed then that's excellent.

If he says actually its worth a bit less then you may have to concede and allow it to sell for that price.

(A surveyor will never put down in his report that he thinks it is worth MORE than the price agreed !)

The problem comes when the property next door has sold within the last month for £ 215,000 you know that from speaking to your neighbour who has just sold it, it has been on the market for six months at £ 225,000,

So on that basis you market yours at £ 220,000, have someone offer you £ 215,000 which you accept happily, then their surveyor says it's only worth £ 190,000.

No matter what you do to try and convince that particular buyer, you are on a loser.

If you are desparate, and the market is poor, seriously consider accepting £ 190,000.

Another person who wants to buy your property may have a surveyor say yes £215,00 is fine, but it may take another six months to get to that stage, another six mortgage payments at least ?

Weigh up the advantages of a low offer no matter how much it hurts your pride, don't be too quick to tell someone to go away !

Accept the offer on condition that the sale goes through quickly & smoothly and you would like it completed by the end of........such and such a date ....in say six or eight weeks time.

Chapter 13

Property Auctions

You may not have ever considered selling your property at auction before, but I would certainly look at the advantages. Originally, it was mainly developers or landlords you had as buyers at auctions, and the properties were repossessions or were not structurally sound.

Now you still get those properties, but a vast array of other property as well. This is becoming a very popular way of selling property, particularly when the property market is poor.

The big advantage of an auction for both sides, both vendor and purchaser, is the speed and efficiency of the process.

Once a final bid is made and the hammer falls (providing it is at the reserve price or higher) the property is sold – SIMPLE

The purchaser has to pay 10% of the purchase price there and then, plus pay the rest within 28 days.

There is no chain of people to worry about, no sleepless nights wondering if the buyer will change their mind.

However the bad news is that not all property gets sold!

In fact at most auctions only 60-70% of the properties entered are sold. This is either because there are no bids on a lot or the more usual case is the fact that the bids received have not achieved the 'Reserve Price' of the property.

Reserve Price

The 'Reserve Price' is the minimum price that the property can be sold for. This is not known to anyone except the vendor and the auctioneer, and has been previously agreed between the auctioneer and vendor a few days before the auction is due. If there has been a lot of interest in the property the reserve price can be set at a reasonably high price. But if there has not been so much interest, then a lower reserve price needs to be set, rather than loose a sale for what may be the sake of a few thousand pounds difference.

Guide Price

The 'Guide Price' is the price put on the auction details, this is kept as low as possible to generate interest in the property. The guide price makes people sit up and take note, the more of a bargain it may seem, the more people will bid, and hopefully drive the price up!

The Auctioneer who conducts the auction is usually a real character, he will laugh and joke with the audience to put them at their ease, convince them that all the properties are good deals, and at the same time try and squeeze the best possible prices out of the people that are attending!

If you visit a property auction, which I recommend you do, you will notice sometimes the guide price is virtually the selling price of a property, give or take a few thousand pounds. On other occasions the auctioneer try as he might cannot solicit a single bid at all on a certain lot. The other case is where a property is bid on by a variety of people and the price keeps going up and up, and you are thinking they must be mad, unless it's your property they are bidding for of course!

Good Auction Properties

The properties that tend to sell well at auctions are……

- ✓ Any property with development or re-development potential, i.e. a property that can be converted into flats, or demolished and have some profitable new property in its place. Property developers and speculators love auctions for this reason !

- ✓ Any dilapidated property with potential

- ✓ If your property is very unique, or unusual and it is not easy to get an idea of price because it can't be compared to a similar property.. ie a windmill, or unusual conversion etc.

- ✓ If your property has structural problems which means it will not get a mortgage on it, or only a small mortgage, meaning the purchaser has to pay CASH in a large amount! This obviously rules out a large amount of prospective purchasers in the normal way of selling.

- ✓ Property that has income, ie small holding, home based business, rental from flats etc.

- ✓ Have you got an amazing USP, a field for grazing, a bit of woodland for getting lost in………..the things dreams are made of!

- ✓ Property with land around it, suitable for extension on a grand scale, with or without planning permission.

✓ Any property that offers a lot for the money !

If you are trying to sell any property such as these please get in touch with an auction company, listed at the back of this book you will find details. Most major Estate Agents have an auction division, or have a company handle property auctions on their behalf.

They will advise you of the suitability of your property for the auction.

It is important to get more than one opinion, so ask at least three auction houses to consider your property. The reputation of the auction company is judged on how successful it is at selling property, so they are not keen on submitting property to auction that has a good chance of NOT selling!

Auction companies can have very regular auctions but there may be a waiting list, and you may have to wait before your property is entered, depending on where you live in the country.

However, the time between the auction catalogue coming out and the auction date is normally under eight weeks, so there is a higher intensity to the selling procedure. The auction company is geared up to focus on every property in the catalogue in readiness for the big day. The phone calls, discussions and viewings are condensed into a very short space of time.

Property auction companies produce far greater quantities of catalogues, and mail them out to more potential buyers than your average Estate Agent. They have mailing lists of these potential buyers, some of which are paying a monthly fee to be sent every catalogue hot off the press. Their web sites are regularly updated, and provide an excellent way for buyers to search for the right property, along with when and where the property is due to be auctioned.

When your property goes in the auction catalogue you may get a lot of people coming to view in a very short space of time, people interested in buying at auction can't waste much time, they have to make a decision to bid or not on the day of the auction. They will also have to sort out their finance and have a survey done before the big day, just in case their bid is successful.

Discuss with the auction companies about doing block viewings on a certain day, or days. This is like an 'Open House' day, but normally far more people turn up this way, and it can be quite surprising to see so many people in one day.

Again it's important to tidy your property up, and be receptive to potential purchasers.

Hand out as many details as possible to every person who views.

Discuss with the auction company your reserve price, this must be the absolute minimum you are prepared to accept, you only get one chance at the auction so think carefully about this.

What is the minimum you need to clear your mortgage and any debts?

Bear in mind that if your property does not sell what price would you be prepared to take in two months time…….or six months time ?

You will be charged an auction fee whether or not your property sells. This needs to be verified with the auction company.

Remember to take into account all the selling fees and solicitors costs.

Also, if you are struggling financially, the benefits of selling your property are not purely financial, health wise to be able to stop worrying and not be as stressed, this is obviously part of the end result.

Ask your agent also about selling with or without planning permission for redevelopment, and the likely delay, but also the saleability of your property.

(A word of warning here……a friend of mine turned down a good offer on his property as he was waiting for the results of a planning application to get permission to build a separate property in the garden, it seemed possible it would be granted as it was a large corner property, however it was refused, and after nine months from the original offer he sold up for a whapping £ 85,000 less ! ……………..so sometimes the lesson is don't be too greedy, a "bird in the hand is worth two in the bush" as the saying goes!)

Right, back to the auction….

Even if you are putting your property in an auction, it does not mean it may not sell before the auction, in the conventional way through your Estate Agent.

The biggest dilemma is to have a prospective purchaser put an offer in before the auction.

The only way is to consider and accept/negotiate a price on condition that contracts are exchanged and completed before the day of the auction – if not then the property goes in the auction.

Otherwise, if your sale falls through you may have to wait another month or so before you can enter the next auction.

Note, the property can be withdrawn at any point normally up until the day of the auction, the auctioneer will read out a list or hand out details of any properties sold / withdrawn for whatever reason prior to the auction starting.

Bad Auction Properties

- × Flats, (or apartments as we seem to call them these days, especially when we are trying to sell them). In good condition or bad, they normally don't reach great prices, especially when the property market is poor.

- × Any house that has had a great deal of money spent on it in recent years and has the usual loft conversion, conservatory, double garage built etc....

Yes, it's the best house in the street, easily worth a lot more than any other in the surrounding streets.........

Unfortunately, not necessarily the case!

When the property market is depressed, and you **"have to sell"** the fact that you spent all that money making your home a little palace does not mean you are going to get all that money back.

It may make someone want your property over another in the same street, but they won't want to pay much more because the market is on their side, they have more choice.

If there are other properties in your street, or other apartments in your block going to auction, or have been to auction, and the guide prices, or selling prices have been less than what you want for your property – forget it.

Your property is very unlikely to beat the trend at an auction, you are better to stick with the traditional methods.

However, if you do put you property in an auction and it does not sell **please don't give up**.

Estate Agents and Auction Houses will tell you that it has damaged the reputation of your property, and been a waste of time, but in reality the fact is that the person who will buy your property has just not appeared yet.

The good news is that if you do sell your property at auction you only have 28 days to get out of the property, so finish off your packing!

Chapter 14

Companies That Buy Houses

You have probably seen them advertised everywhere...............

We will buy your house now!

Instant decision!

Completion within seven days!

So what's the catch?

These companies operate in different ways…..

They will buy properties that are normally good sellers in a 'normal' property market, what Estate agents call 'bread & butter' properties……

They are looking at the market long term, five to ten years, and in the mean time they will rent the properties out.

They have a certain price, for example...for a three bedroom semi in a certain area, regardless of the fact it may have an expensive kitchen, or a larger garden than most.

Remember this is business, they are not swayed by your wonderful garden of roses or the fact you are leaving the washing machine!

They are not going to live there.

As a guide, on average they pay 20 to 30% LESS than the market value.

What the market value actually is can be a cause for debate.

Yes, this is why they will buy your house within seven days !

Some of these companies will buy your property and allow you to rent it back off them.

This is ideal for anyone who has a lot of equity in their property, and perhaps got in to debt, or behind with their mortgage payments, but likes where they live.

It may be the monthly rent you end up paying is less than the monthly mortgage payments you were struggling with. Plus, you have the added peace of mind that if something goes wrong like a blocked drain or a slate blows off the roof , then all you have to do is telephone your landlord, it is not you who pays for the maintenance problems any more, so you save money this way also, and added peace of mind.

Plus you have some cash to put in the bank !

So, please consider this option, there is no harm in contacting some of these companies and sounding them out.

By all means speak to other people they have dealt with and other former owners who are now their tenants, about any problems or complaints.

Just make sure you use some common sense, and your solicitor is involved at every step.

Obviously, if you do become their tenant you will have a proper tenancy agreement, this will state a certain term which is subject to renewal, and allows both you to leave as tenant providing you give notice, and likewise for the landlord to serve notice on you if he wants vacant possession of the property to sell it, or do something else in the future, so there are no guarantees on either side.

It is possible to get some agreement to give you at least a certain minimum time in the property as a condition of you letting them have it at a certain 'good price'.

It may prove to be the ideal solution – provided everything is done properly.

Some of these companies act as agents, and just pass your details on to another company or private investor for a fee, or a percentage depending on the type of property, or area it is in.

Best types of property for this

Low cost, easily rentable, FTB property…..

Small flats/ apartments

Small houses

They don't have to be anything special, just the properties that are reasonably cheap to purchase, and give a good rental return.

Similar Companies

If you are a Senior Citizen....Equity Release Schemes

They have been around for a long time, and also got a bit of bad press, but don't dismiss them straight away.

These companies will effectively buy your house off you, and then allow you to stay in the property until you die, the money they offer you will reflect this fact.

The advantage here, compared to the other companies we have mentioned is that the contract you sign states this fact, at no point can they ask you to find somewhere else.

Yes, they are hoping you won't live to be 120, but if you do they can't do anything about it.

When you do depart this life, then your property is theirs, and whether it is worth twice what they paid you for it, or half what they paid... so be it.

Again be careful and get some good advice.

If you don't have any relatives, or ones you don't particularly want to inherit your palace, then to be able to stay put and have extra cash to go on some good holidays, or pay for medical treatment, or distribute some inheritance early….. it's your choice.

Chapter 15

Raffle It!!

This seems to be the answer for some people !

However, the legalities of raffling off your property are not exactly straightforward.

How it should be done......

Firstly, you should take advice from the Gaming Association, a Solicitor and an Accountant, and try to understand the legalities of doing this.

To comply with the law it needs to be a 'Competition' with some degree of skill and the entrants need to pay.

You really need to set up a web site, charge £20 to £30 per ticket, stipulate how many tickets need to be sold to cover the value of your property and the costs of the competition, then have a relevant competition question for each entrant to answer. State when the competition will close and the draw take place.

You need to publicise the competition in newspapers and generate as much good publicity as possible to sell the tickets.

This is the main problem, how do you sell literally thousands of tickets ?

Well get a good web site produced, donate a percentage to charity, try and do all you can to make everything 'above board' !

The main reason a lot of people do not reach the target of tickets required is due to the general public being sceptical about the way the competition is being run. The odds of winning may be much greater than playing the lottery, but if you do not get enough entrants there is always a chance of no-one winning the property and only giving out a cash prize instead, or handing the money back, or you running off with the cash !

So good publicity is the key and you need lots of it.

The most successful competition I know about was the house with fishing lake and holiday lodges in Devon worth a cool £ 1 million, the owners managed to sell the target of 46,000 tickets at £ 25.00 each, totalling £ 1.15 million, allowing for costs and stamp duty. Perhaps the more a property is worth, the more desirable it is as a competition prize!

The normal length of time to have the competition open for is about six months, with an option to extend if the target number of tickets has not been reached.

If you are miles away from your target after six months then it may be best to just hold the draw and give the money raised as a cash prize. You are not allowed to make a profit out of this competition, but you can keep enough money to cover your costs.

There are some recent companies that offer the service to 'raffle' your house, but it is early days yet, and none seem to get a great deal of publicity.

If you know anyone 'famous' who could help promote your house competition, or a TV programme etc so much the better.

You may be able to get someone from a charity you are donating a percentage to, in order to give you some publicity.

Andrew Dale

Chapter 16

Swap or Part-Exchange

Can you swap your property, or ideally swap for something smaller and get some cash as well?

This does involve some effort on your part, and some deep thinking………

Just sit down with a blank peace of paper and a pen and daydream, however silly some of the options you have pop into your mind, you must write them down!

This can be amazingly effective if done well.

Let me explain in more detail…….

If you are relatively young i.e. under 50! and have a bungalow, or perhaps a ground floor flat, why not try and find someone like a retired couple with a larger house that perhaps needs some work, and is difficult for them to go up and down stairs at their age…..surely they would consider a straight swap or perhaps for them to give you an amount to cover any difference in agreed price!

I know this sounds unlikely, but you would be surprised how this sort of arrangement can cut out the hassle and pressure and uncertainty on both sides. Plus why don't you offer to help with moving their furniture etc as a good will gesture.

It Works

Some friends of ours put their house up for sale and when they got chatting with a couple who came to view and liked their house, the viewing couple lived in a bungalow, just around the corner and what do you know….

Hey presto ! They bought each others properties……….

The advantage was firstly, no chain, they could both decide when they wanted to move, in this case just after Christmas, to make things easier for both parties.

Secondly, they both got the property they wanted, and didn't have far to move either!

More ideas

The other idea is to swap or part exchange for something easier to sell, usually with a bit of work, or a new kitchen and bathroom etc.

OR a property that can generate additional income without much difficulty.

Yes, this chapter is a bit of a wild card, but there may be someone you already know, or a property you have driven past this morning that has a possibility.

There are web sites, and adverts in your local newspaper, and why not advertise yourself…. Example below…

Luxury ground floor Apartment, Belgravia District

recently valued at £250,000 No Chain

Owner open to offers around £ 230,000, or may swap or Part Ex,

Anything considered… please give me a quick call…..

Andrew 07788 911 888

Speak to the estate agents about this and most of the time they are not interested, because it is not straight forward, the idea off trying to negotiate something a bit more difficult is not welcomed. But don't give up, anyone who comes to view your property, ask if they may be interested in a swap or part exchange!

New developments

Look at the back pages of your local paper on the day property is the main feature, if you go to the section on new developments you will see the large enticing adverts of major developers who want you to buy their latest 'must have' property, 'only two remaining' absolutely the best place to live !!!!

Anyway look for the adverts that say 'part exchange considered' or 'we will buy your present home'

The point is that some of these developers are capable of coming up with amazing ways of selling their property, they will bend over backwards, and do some amazing deals to get their development sold!

Especially if times are difficult, or even if they have nearly sold most of the development and only have a few units left, they very often just want to finish and move on.

Another friend of ours who was struggling to sell his house for over twelve months and then one day he was looking through a newspaper he had picked up when he had visit the area he had decided he wanted to retire to, and there it was…….

An advert for a new development of bungalows in Hampshire, close to the New Forest, a mile from where he had been on holiday may times with his wife and guess what…….Part-Exchange Considered !

To cut to the chase it worked, and they ended up with a lovely detached bungalow, ideal for their retirement.

Andrew Dale

Chapter 17

The Alternatives

If the main reason you want to move is purely down to money, and you are struggling to make ends meet, you may not have to sell if you don't want to, the other possibilities that you can consider are the following….

Rent-a-room scheme…..

Did you know you can take in a lodger to rent one of your rooms, charge up to about £ 80.00 per week, and you pay no tax on this income. (Not many people know about this)

Has a friend or relative or someone at work got a sale going through on their property and needs somewhere temporary to stay? Will they pay you £80 a week until they find somewhere ?

Rent out your garage for storage

You would not believe the amount of people who are looking for storage…. You can easily get £10 to £15 a week for a single garage, and £ 25 a week for a double garage.

Rent your land

Space to store a touring caravan, £ 10 a week per caravan.

If you have a large garden / field then could you let horses to graze on it (£ 10 a week per horse)

Sell your land

Can you just sell off part of your property or land, with or without planning permission.

Rent the whole house

Could you rent out your whole house, and then rent a smaller cheaper property for six to twelve months, whilst you wait and see if the property market picks up or your financial situation changes. In a difficult property market the demand for rental property increases.

The point is there may have been ideas that have crossed your mind in the past about other ways you could make some extra money from where you live, but you have never really pursued them because you didn't have the time, or you couldn't really be bothered !

Well, now you may have too !

Plus there are many other home based businesses that you can start without much money or time just to make some extra money, and make ends meet.

Andrew Dale

More Useful Information

Main UK Property Selling Websites...

Rightmove.co.uk

Zoopla.co.uk

Findaproperty.com

Primelocation.com

Companies that buy houses....

Thepropertybuyers.co.uk

Repossession-Stoppers.com

Sellpropertyfast-uk.co.uk

Property Auction Information......

Eigroup.co.uk

Propertyauctionzone.com

UK House Builders who offer Part-Exchange Schemes...

Taylorwimpey.co.uk

Persimmonhomes.com

Barratthomes.co.uk

Redrow.co.uk

Other sites to check-out...............

Nethouseprices.com

Preloved.co.uk

Propertysnake.co.uk

Goodschoolsguide.co.uk

Homestagingconsultants.co.uk

Two Amazing Books To Inspire You……….

"The Power of Positive Thinking"

by

Norman Vincent Peale

"How to Win Friends & Influence People"

by

Dale Carnegie

Printed in Great Britain
by Amazon.co.uk, Ltd.,
Marston Gate.